JORDAN

TIGER BOOKS INTERNATIONAL

Text by
Nino Gorio

Graphic design
Anna Galliani

Map
Cristina Franco

Contents

The liveliness of the desert....................................*page 28*
In the shadow of temples and minarets.................*page 54*
People of fields and camels.................................*page 70*
A legend called history...*page 88*

1 *The deep valley of Wadi Rum is one of the most famous and popular spots in the Jordanian desert. Wedged between sheer walls of rock in the south of the country, towards Saudi Arabia, it is surrounded by the highest peaks in the land – Jebel Rum (5,754 feet) and Jebel Umm 'Ishrin (5,751 feet). The Jordanians consider it a symbol of their country's independence; during the First World War, Lawrence of Arabia's Bedouin guerrillas set up their base here before the attack on the stronghold of Aqaba, which was crucial to the expulsion of the Turks from Jordan.*

2-3 *Almost nine-tenths of Jordanian territory are classified as "arid and unproductive". However, the desert can work miracles at times; the rocks of Wadi Rum are parched and inhospitable at first sight, but numerous springs are concealed among them. An aquifer also runs beneath the sand, fairly close to the surface, allowing the growth of various shrubs and grasses. For this reason the gorge is inhabited by Bedouins, who raise goats and dromedaries there. In ancient times the valley was known for its relative abundance of water; in the pre-Roman period the caravan trail between Yemen and Palestine (the "Incense Road") passed this way, although the coastal route would have been shorter.*

4-5 *With only some 20 miles of coastline, Jordan's sole outlet to the Red Sea is postage-stamp sized. However, this short stretch of coast wedged between Israel, Saudi Arabia and the mountains has everything: a city (Aqaba, shown in the photo) with an important harbour, beaches, and even a nature reserve.*

6-7 *Few Arab countries can boast an architectural heritage to match Jordan's. To the north, in Roman times, stood Decapolis, a league of 10 cities, of which eloquent ruins remain. The largest are those of Jerash (the ancient Gerasa) which reached the height of its splendour in the 3rd century.*

8 *The most important archaeological site in Jordan is Petra, the former Nabataean capital excavated in rock in the Mounts of Edom, which was conquered in A.D. 106 by the Emperor Trajan. The most impressive monument in Petra is ad-Deir ("the Monastery"), a temple 150 feet tall; this photo shows the tholos, the typical circular sanctuary on the façade.*

9 *The main access route to Petra is through the Siq, a canyon crossed on foot, which emerges opposite al-Khazneh ("the Treasure"), a mausoleum dating from the 1st century B.C. that suddenly appears, brightly silhouetted beyond the shadow of the gorge.*

This edition published in 1997 by TIGER BOOKS INTERNATIONAL PLC , 26a York Street Twickenham TW1 3LJ, England.

First published by Edizioni White Star. Title of the original edition: Giordania, Paese di deserti, castelli e profeti. © World copyright 1997 by Edizioni White Star, Via Candido Sassone 22/24, 13100 Vercelli, Italy.

ISBN 1-85501-918-3

Printed in Singapore by Tien Wah Press.
Colour separations by Magenta Lithographic Con.

MEDITERRANEAN
SEA

PELLA

JERASH

Jordan

ZARQA

SALT

AMMAN

EL AZRAQ

JERUSALEM

▲ Mt. Nebo
MADABA

Dead
Sea

KARAK

ISRAEL

EGYPT

Wadi Araba

M O A B

▲ Mt. Edom

PETRA

RUM

▲ Jebel Rum
5,754

AQABA

Gulf of Aqaba

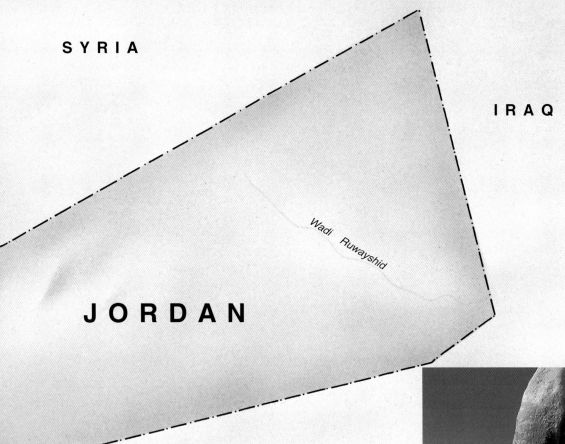

SYRIA

IRAQ

Wadi Ruwayshid

JORDAN

a' ir

11 *As you travel south or away from the River Jordan, the landscape changes dramatically after a few dozen miles, and parched land predominates once more. In the Jordanian desert, which is mainly stony, the rocks have been dramatically modelled by atmospheric agents. A good example is this natural arch on Jebel Al-Khubthah which frames the Corinthian Tomb, one of the best-known Hellenistic monuments in Petra.*

12-13 *The original stock of the Jordanian population are the Bedouins, descendants of nomadic tribes who made their living by stock rearing. The officers of the Desert Police Patrol, who patrol the remotest areas on camels, are recruited from Bedouin tribes. The Desert Police wear the traditional red-and-white* keffiyeh *with their green uniforms.*

14-15 *The capital, Amman, is a modern city which has undergone a dramatic population explosion in the last few decades; its population has increased from under 300,000 to around one and a half million inhabitants.*

16-17 *Impossible as it may seem, the desert is never wholly uninhabited; some 5,000 Bedouins live in the lonely Wadi Rum valley.*

SAUDI
ARABIA

Introduction

One winter's day many years ago, a strange character was roaming through the Mounts of Edom in southern Jordan. Although the man rode an Arab steed and wore a Bedouin *keffiyeh*, he was blonde-haired and carried a Swiss passport in the name of Johann Ludwig Burckhardt. He entered a narrow canyon between pink sandstone walls, rode on for a mile, came out in a wide rocky hollow and nearly fell off his horse from excitement. There, in that remote valley, the whole of the mountain had been carved by man, centuries earlier, into tombs, temples and staircases. Burckhardt had rediscovered Petra, the "rose-red city half as old as time", of which the Crusaders had told fabulous tales.

It was 1812, and the Mounts of Edom were still ruled by the Turkish sultans, jealous custodians of all the secrets of the East. Another century was to pass before the discovery of the strange *keffiyeh*-wearing Swiss traveller could be studied, in 1920. But now, Petra has become a star; some years ago it was used as a set for an Indiana Jones film, and every day it attracts thousands of tourists, following in Burkhardt's footsteps in their luxury coaches. As a result its most famous monuments, Ed-Deyr (Sanctuary) and Khazneh (Treasure) are now part and parcel of the image of Jordan, like King Hussein's moustache and the surreal walls of Wadi Rum, the desert of Lawrence of Arabia.

However, Jordan does not only mean Petra. The country is large, though not enormous; it has an area of about 35.56 square miles (three times the size of Belgium) according to the most realistic figures, which do not include the West Bank, lost in the Six-Day War in 1967. It seems even vaster to those who cross it, perhaps because it is occupied to the east by desert plateaux, where it is easy to lose your sense of distance. To the west the horizon is narrower, because the world precipitates into the Ghor, the deep depression in the earth's crust which stretches from the Jordan Valley through the Dead Sea to Wadi Arabah, a rift that runs for a distance of 190 miles, all below sea level.

Jordan is a strange land. This is a country whose maps show a great lake where none exists (there are only two small ones because the Dead Sea has dried up in the middle); a country which is 87% desert, with a population of only 4 million, but manages to raise 3 million sheep, horses and cows; a country which has 490 miles of railways (more than Israel), but 18,000 camels too. A country which in wartime locates the King's residence (at Aqaba) 165 feet from the enemy's border; which promotes peace with Israel but rejects the UN embargo against Iraq; which was only founded in 1946, but has a 9,000-year-old history.

In order to understand this strange land, you need to travel down north-west of Petra; down from the Mounts of Edom, steeply down by gorges and rock walls to sea level, and then down still further, into the bottomless pit of the Ghor, to the lowest point on earth: 1,280 feet below sea level. Right at the bottom, where the retreating Dead Sea

has left behind black mud and weird pinnacles of salt, Sodom and Gomorrah once stood. According to the Bible, these towns were burnt down by God because they were so sinful. No-one knows exactly where they were; Sodom is usually said to have been located just over the Israeli border, though there is no proof of this, while no trace has ever been found of Gomorrah.

What had the two towns done to deserve this fate? Nothing very different from other populations in the region: they pastured their goats, worshipped Astarte, the goddess of love, and had rather more liberal sexual customs than the Jews. But that's not the point; those who wrote about Sodom and Gomorrah were people who looked out on the Dead Sea from the opposite shore – from the olive groves and green fields of Judæa, the outpost of the Mediterranean. For the people of the West, the Ghor constitutes an imaginary frontier, where green fields end and the boundless, magical world of the Arab deserts begins. This is a different, mysterious world that is both intriguing and frightening – just like sin.

Sodom and Gomorrah were the outpost and symbol of the other half of the world – the arid, endless stretch of land from which not only rare spices and exotic perfumes, but also hungry nomadic tribes, insidious foreign cults and proud enemy armies travelled to the West by unknown routes. The land we call Jordan has always constituted the gateway to that vague, nebulous East in which the Bible confined those from whom the Jews preferred to set themselves apart: Ishmael, father of the Arabs, the son of Abraham and a slave-girl; Esau, father of the Edomites, who sold his birthright for a mess of pottage, and Moab, father of the Moabites, born of an incestuous relationship between Lot and one of his daughters.

Jordan has borne this stigma for 3,000 years, and over the centuries many have tried to seal it up in its deserts, surrounding it with barriers. Go to the frontier post at the Allenby Bridge and look over to the other side; above Jericho stands the ancient fortress called Kiprus, the stronghold of a line of fortifications built by Herod the Great (the "King of the Jews" referred to in the Gospels) to keep his eastern neighbours at a safe distance. Others tried before and after Herod, including the Seleucids, Syrian heirs of Alexander the Great, the Romans, who ventured well beyond the River Jordan (they built the forts of Azraq and Al-Hallabat to the east of Amman), and the Crusaders (castle of Al-Karak).

Remote history? Not at all: the Israeli wire that runs along the Ghor, and has been impassable for half a century, is none other than a modern Kiprus, the last effect of the barrier (more cultural than military) erected against Gomorrah. Yet barbarians have never lived across the Jordan, only a population that might be restless and annoying, but has given the world lessons in civilisation, as demonstrated not only by Petra, but also by thousands of other lesser-known sites. Al-Baydah, for example, is the oldest known village in the world; it is in fact 9,000 years old and only stones remain there. It gives you the creeps – this was where man learned to have houses, fields and roots. Europe did not follow suit until 30 centuries later.

In the long run, however, the various Kipruses of history have been a good thing. Thanks to the barriers that sealed up the country for so long, Jordan is now a huge open-air museum, where all the signs of a magnificent culture – archaeological remains, customs and place names – have remained untouched. For example, Biblical populations like the Edomites, Ammonites and Moabites are legendary names to us, but here they are a reality, written on the map: the Mounts of Edom encircle Petra, Amman is the capital, and Moab is an oasis on the River Jordan. Incredibly enough, these names have remained unchanged for 3,000 years.

In Amman, the (true) story of an animal is told as a parable of this survival. This is how it goes. Once upon a time there was (and indeed still is) the desert wolf; slightly smaller and redder than the one that appears in our fairytales, it once lived everywhere, hunting gazelles. Then everything changed; the desert was criss-crossed by roads, the stony ground was interrupted by vegetable gardens, and springs were diverted to provide village water supplies. The wolves were confined to Azraq, in the far East of the country near the Iraq border. There were no gazelles there, only mice and partridges; no springs, only basalt hollows where rainwater collected. A death sentence? No, Azraq was the salvation of the desert wolves; this isolation allowed them to survive, whereas their cousins further west were wiped out by a world that would not accept them.

What happened to Jordanian culture is rather like the story of those wolves; isolation saved it. It is no accident that the main custodians of the country's memories and traditions are the Jordanians who live (or did until not long ago) more isolated than the rest: the Bedouins, nomadic shepherds of Arab stock who live in the desert. Simple and proud, romanticised or despised with no half measures, they are by no means found only in Jordan; the typical black tents, women's embroidered veils and flocks of goats grazing on nothing are signs of their presence all over the Middle East – in Saudi Arabia, Egypt, Israel, Syria and Iraq. However, the Bedouin country par excellence is Jordan. Only a few details are needed to prove this statement. Half the inhabitants of Jordan belong to or are descended from tribes of shepherds, such as the Howeitat, Beni Attiya, Beni Khalid, Beni Sakhr, Shiran and Beni Hassan tribes. The Royal Guard, the hand-picked corps which protects the reigning sovereign in Amman, consists wholly of Bedouins, as does the Desert Police Force, whose officers patrol the loneliest areas wearing the characteristic *khaki* uniform and red-and-white *keffiyeh*.

The *keffiyeh* is the headgear of all Arabs; in Jordan, the red-and-white *keffiyeh* is the badge of the "natives", while the other half of the population, who are of Palestinian descent, usually wear the black-and-white *keffiyeh*. However, the difference between the two peoples does not only lie in the *keffiyeh*; the Bedouins, at least the most traditionalist, have very different customs from other Jordanians in all spheres of life. This applies to etiquette: in their tents they eat without cutlery and only with the right hand; using the left hand is considered an affront. It applies to work: if a Bedouin becomes sedentary he will prefer to work as a craftsman (silver and carpet making) rather than a farmer. It applies to the family: polygamy is allowed, but it is the first wife who chooses her husband's new brides. It applies to minor details: a Jordanian shepherd prefers coffee to tea,

18 top *Jordanian handicrafts are varied and imaginative, though not as commercially well-known as those of other Arab countries, such as Morocco leather and Yemeni jewellery. The country's traditional crafts include carpet weaving, now mainly carried on in modern workshops like this one, on the slopes of Mount Nebo.*

18 bottom *The Bedouins who live in the areas of Al-Tafilah, Al-Karak, Madaba, Wadi Rum and Disah are masters of the art of carpet weaving. Their favourite raw material is goat's wool. The weavers are nearly always women.*

19 *The value of a carpet is based on many factors, especially the density of the knots, which depends on the weaver's skill and patience. An efficient loom is not enough to obtain a good product.*

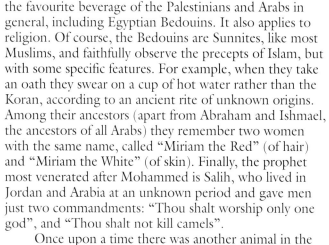

the favourite beverage of the Palestinians and Arabs in general, including Egyptian Bedouins. It also applies to religion. Of course, the Bedouins are Sunnites, like most Muslims, and faithfully observe the precepts of Islam, but with some specific features. For example, when they take an oath they swear on a cup of hot water rather than the Koran, according to an ancient rite of unknown origins. Among their ancestors (apart from Abraham and Ishmael, the ancestors of all Arabs) they remember two women with the same name, called "Miriam the Red" (of hair) and "Miriam the White" (of skin). Finally, the prophet most venerated after Mohammed is Salih, who lived in Jordan and Arabia at an unknown period and gave men just two commandments: "Thou shalt worship only one god", and "Thou shalt not kill camels".

Once upon a time there was another animal in the Jordanian deserts, apart from the wolf, with which the Bedouins liked to identify: the *maha* (Arabian oryx). This is an antelope with a white coat and straight horns so parallel that, seen from the side, they look like a single horn. This is how the legend of the unicorn, which the Crusaders claimed to have seen in the East, originated in the Middle Ages. The *maha* is a champion of survival: it can travel 90 miles a day in search of food, and go without water for 11 months. It is the ideal symbol for the Bedouins, in whose eyes the ability to survive in the desert is synonymous with manly independence. The inhabitants of this land have always been proud, independent and different, since long before they were called Jordanians. It therefore comes as no surprise to discover that the desert tribes looked with suspicion not only on the people of the West, but also on many of their "brothers in Islam".

The Omayyads, caliphs of Damascus, built the *qasr* (castles) of Amrah and At-Tubah, to the south-east of Amman, in the 8th century, when the Koran already united Syria with the nomads of the south. The Ottomans, sultans of Turkey, who ruled for four centuries (from 1517 to 1918), did even more: they built an extensive network of garrisons in the country, which ran as far as the *qasr* of Aqaba, on the Red Sea. However, keeping imitators of the *maha* under control is no easy task; how can you "seal in" people used to considering the desert as their home and borders as meaningless? So at every attempt to isolate them, the Jordanians react with an equal tendency to travel, trade and look beyond their frontiers.

This has always happened. Three roads cross the country from north to south: to the right runs the Desert Highway, to the left the Arabah Highway, and in the middle, the King's Highway. The first is now the busiest, but the third is the oldest; for centuries it was the most important caravan route in the Middle East, a bridge between the desert and the rest of the world. Before the invention of the motor car, millions of anonymous camels and a great deal of history (not only Jordanian) travelled along that road, which runs from Petra to Amman (the turn-off for Damascus and Jerusalem). Moses travelled this way on his journey from Egypt to the Promised Land; later came the Byzantine armies of Justinian, heading south, and the armies of Mohammed's father-in-law, Abu Bakr, heading north. If you follow the former caravan route you will find traces of all these events: the Exodus is commemorated on

19

Mounts Nebo and Harun by two mausoleums, where Moses and his brother Aaron are said to be buried; the Byzantines by the famous mosaics of Madaba, and Abu Bakr by the thousand minarets of a land which has remained Islamic since his day.

However, the King's Highway was not invented by Moses, still less by Justinian or Abu Bakr. It already existed, with the same name, 3,500 years ago. Its origins date back to the Bronze Age, and are associated with a resin considered sacred in the ancient world, which the Arabs call *luban* and we call incense. It can have various colours, from yellow to purple, but is always obtained from the *boswellia*, a tree that only grows in the distant lands of Yemen and Oman. On the strength of their monopoly those countries did a roaring trade in incense from time immemorial: caravans laden with *luban* crossed the Arabian Peninsula heading for Jordan, and then branched off to the various markets, especially in Egypt and Syria. This is how the King's Highway began, as a path beaten by nomads carrying incense north.

The most original civilisation to inhabit these regions prospered as a result of the trade in incense, for centuries more precious than gold. This was the civilisation of the Nabataeans, known as the "lords of the desert", who first unified what is now Jordan, making it a strong, independent kingdom (between the 1st century B.C. and the 1st century A.D.). The Nabataeans were Arabs; originally shepherds, they later became shrewd merchants, farmers, potters and architects. Under King Aretas III (87-62 B.C.) they came to rule Damascus, but the heart of the kingdom was always the desert, where mountains sacred to the god Dushara encircled a capital with a magical name: Petra. Which brings us back to where we came in, with the "rose-red city" on the Mounts of Edom.

Petra can be reached by many roads, with many vehicles, but the last mile must be covered on foot along the Siq, the narrow canyon down which Burckhardt rode. This is the best way to appreciate one of the most famous views in the Middle East: the silhouette of the Khazneh, set ablaze by the sun, which suddenly bursts into the shadow of the canyon. The Khazneh is the "visiting card" of Petra; it is excavated in the rock face with impressive statues and columns, and was perhaps a temple or a royal mausoleum. Further on, the same pattern is repeated ad infinitum; 800 monuments have so far been discovered in the valley, and the work is still continuing.

Not everything there is Nabataean, because Petra was Roman by the time of its decline. However, the most beautiful temples date back to the golden years of Aretas IV (9 B.C. -A.D. 39); the "rose-red city" flourished under his reign as Florence did under Lorenzo de' Medici. Though powerful and sophisticated, Nabataean Petra, the crossroads of the incense routes, long overshadowed the Roman cities of the North – Gerasa (now Jarash), Pella and Gadara (now Umm Qays). Then, in A.D. 106, Rome gained the upper hand, and the kings of *luban* made their exit from the historical scene. However, 17 centuries later, at the time of Burckhardt, they were still there, not called Nabataeans but Liyatneh; they had reverted to being Bedouin shepherds, as they had been since time immemorial, and still lived in the ruins of the former capital.

Petra constitutes a link that connects the past and present of this land. For example, the guerrilla warfare that was to lead to the expulsion of the Turks and the birth of modern Jordan began in these very mountains in 1916. For Europeans, the leading figure of this period was an Englishman: T.E. Lawrence, otherwise known as Lawrence of Arabia. But for Arabs, the real protagonist was Hussein Ibn Ali, Emir of Mecca and sheikh of the Hashemites, a noble branch of the Quraysh tribe; a descendent of Mohammed and the great-grandfather of the present King Hussein. It was he who incited the Bedouins to revolt; they would never have followed an infidel without the blessing of the charismatic Emir.

The present-day Jordanians have named roads, squares and a mosque in Amman after Hussein. Lawrence is commemorated by a spring in one of the loveliest parts of the southern desert: Wadi Rum, a dreamy valley situated between the highest mountains in the country, Jebel Ram (5,754 feet) and Umm 'Ishrin (5,751 feet). These are familiar names to anyone who has read *The Seven Pillars of Wisdom*, Lawrence's autobiography; the British agent set up his base with Feysal, the son of Emir Hussein, amid the impressive scenery of Wadi Rum, "a processional route that defies the imagination". The attack on the *qasr* of Aqaba, the turning point in the war against the Turks, was launched from there.

When the Turks were defeated there was great rejoicing, but not for all; at the same time, while the whole country was swarming with armed men, the *maha*, the antelope adopted as their symbol by the Bedouins, became extinct. However, Arab countries were rising from the ashes of the Ottoman Empire. The birth of Jordan was long and difficult: after the war, in 1921, Hussein's oldest son (Abdullah) found himself ruling a British protectorate (Transjordan), which did not become independent until 1946, and took its present name in 1949. The rest is recent history: the wars with Israel (1948-49, 1967 and 1973), the annexation of the West Bank (1949) and its loss (1967), and finally, the recent peace.

Peace – so long awaited, so attractive, but so controversial. Remember? It broke out at 2 p.m. on 26th October 1994 when King Hussein shook hands with Yitzhak Rabin on the border between Aqaba and Eilat, reopened after half a century. That day, the sky was filled with coloured balloons, never seen before against the yellow background of the Negev desert. It seemed like a miracle, and the people expected many more miracles from that event. Ambitious projects were already being planned: a pipeline from the Mediterranean to bring water to the Dead Sea, which is drying up; artificial tributaries to make the River Jordan as large as the Euphrates; and finally an International Peace Park, to be constructed at Wadi Araba.

But the real miracle has already been performed, and its name is Jordan. Visitors who travel beyond the Ghor today can hardly believe that the country didn't exist 60 years ago; they find clean towns, well-kept roads and newly restored monuments. Amman is one of the most orderly Arab capitals, although it is growing at an astonishing rate: it had 570,000 inhabitants in 1970, whereas now there are 1,900,000. Then there are the cultivated areas; these had

always existed by the River Jordan, but fields and vegetable gardens are also springing up in the desert, on such a scale that citrus fruit, tomatoes and olive oil are now exported. Schools are also being built; Jordan has the highest literacy rate in the Arab world (81%), on a par with the Lebanon and the Emirates.

The results are all the more surprising in view of the fact that the country has virtually no oil, the treasure trove of half the Middle East (it produces 35,000 times less than the Emirates), and that half a century of independence has not been at all easy. In addition to three wars with Israel, the economy has had to cope with three waves of refugees, two from Palestine, in 1948 and 1967, and the last from Iraq in 1990, just before the Gulf War. The third wave, less well-known than the others, was the most onerous: 800,000 refugees flooded into Jordan in just a few days, right at the time when the anti-Saddam embargo was ruining Jordanian business with Iraq, which had always been its trading partner.

The effects of that crisis are still being felt, together with some tension, but the country's medium-term development is still surprising. The instigator of this development is a well-known figure in Europe: Hussein Ibn Talal, the Hashemite king who has ruled the country since 1952. King Hussein is not only the great-grandson of Emir Hussein (and therefore a descendent of the Prophet Mohammed), but also an old boy of prestigious English boarding schools; he is a king who wears both *keffiyeh* and tie, and not only in the metaphorical sense. The country is like him: it is Arabic to the core and jealous of its traditions, but also looks beyond Kiprus, like the ancient Nabataeans. If this guideline is remembered, many apparent paradoxes will be seen to be merely logical choices.

This is a wholeheartedly Arabian country whose population flocks to the beaches fully dressed, as required by the Koran, on Friday, the day of rest; a country that sublimates its desire for the nomadic life in long lines of trucks – the caravans of the modern world – heading from Aqaba to Baghdad; a country that refused peace with Israel until the Palestinians signed the treaty and which, though moderate, rejected the embargo against Iraq, which is considered to represent interference with the internal affairs of another country. It is also a country receptive to anything good originating outside its borders: it has copied the British multi-party parliamentary system, and is capable of shaking its former enemies by the hand and then keeping its word.

We will close our account of Jordan with a surprise. Take the road leading to Iraq, but turn south at Azraq, to a place called Shawmari. There, amid acacias and *wadis*, you will come across a herd of elegant white antelopes with long, straight horns. They are oryx, the symbols of the Bedouins, which became extinct 90 years ago. Another miracle? Yes, but it was performed by the Royal Jordanian Society for the Conservation of Nature, the agency responsible for the country's parks and nature reserves.

The offspring of a pair which had survived in a zoo, these oryx were reaccustomed to the desert and then released. Now they live, run free and multiply in the place where the wolves once found peace, free and proud, like the great-grandchildren of Miriam the Red.

The liveliness of the desert

28 top *Most of the country is situated on plateaux, where desolate gorges alternate with chains of rocky mountains. The tallest peak in Jordan (Jebel Rum), whose sheer walls reach stand 5,800 feet high, looms over Wadi Rum.*

28 bottom *Rocks are the characteristic feature of the Jordanian desert. The ancient Romans called the region Arabia Petraea, a play on words; Petra was the capital of this remote province of the Empire, and the land was petrosus (full of stones). However, despite the prevalence of rocks and the colour ochre, a touch of greenery can be seen here and there; various plant species such as Hamada salicornica (shown in this photo) have adapted to the arid climate and its wide temperature ranges. Even fig trees, which have perhaps grown from seeds carried on the wind, can sometimes be seen in the middle of the desert, near perennial springs.*

29 *The mountains of the Jordanian desert are varied in terms of geological characteristics. The main types of rock in the centre and south of the country are limestone and pinkish-ochre sandstone (shown in the photo), which give the landscape dolomitic characteristics. Elsewhere, especially in the north-east, basalts and lavas of much darker, more violent colours are found.*

Wadi Rum, the ochre-tinted valley of myths and legends

30 *"A processional route that defies the imagination" was how Lawrence of Arabia described Wadi Rum, the impressive gorge wedged between the mountains to the north-east of Aqaba, towards Saudi Arabia. T. E. Lawrence, the controversial British agent who fought side by side with the Arab rebels of Emir Hussein I from 1916 to 1918, used this area as the base for his guerrilla warfare against the Turks. This is where he planned his memoirs, later entitled "The Seven Pillars of Wisdom".*

31 top *Wadi Rum is relatively well supplied with springs and grass, so it has always been a necessary halt for caravans crossing the Arabian Desert from south to north. Already inhabited in the epi-Palaeolithic period (20,000-10,000 B.C.), the valley acquired strategic importance in the first millennium B.C. when there was a flourishing trade in spices and incense between Sheba (present-day Yemen) and Petra, from which Sheban products were sent to the Egyptian and Phoenician markets.*

31 bottom *The sunsets of Wadi Rum are famous; when the sun sinks below the horizon, lengthening the shadows and highlighting every feature of the terrain, the colour of the limestone rocks turns to warm, amber shades. It was the magic of such places that gave rise to the legend of the djinns, the genies which, according to tradition, live in the desert. The conviction that djinns really exist is so strong that even Mohammed, the intransigent enemy of animism, admitted their existence.*

32 *The impressive walls of Jebel Khazali close the main branch of Wadi Rum to the south. Around the mountain there is nothing but dry sand, and a canyon (Siq Khazali), runs between the rocks. This place has been considered sacred since prehistoric times; the walls of the Siq are covered with carvings, probably votive offerings by goatherds to thank the gods for the unexpected gift received.*

33 *The Wadi Rum trail evokes a thousand stories verging on legends; Bilqis, the Queen of Sheba, who according to the Bible and the Koran travelled to Jerusalem around 950 B.C. to visit King Solomon, passed this way. But non-Arabs have always looked fearfully on these valleys; a Roman army was lost here, and the few survivors reported that monsters and dragons lived in the region.*

34-35 *Seen from the air, the Arabian Desert appears in all its extraordinary, desolate immensity along the Jordanian-Saudi border. The rainfall in this area never exceeds 50 millimetres a year, and sometimes no more than 8-10 mm falls. The temperature fluctuates wildly; on winter nights it can fall to -14°C, while in summer it often reaches 50° in the shade. It is not unusual for these parched mountains to be covered with snow in the harder winters.*

36-37 *Now, Wadi Rum is a protected nature reserve, which tourists can only enter if accompanied by a guide – on foot, in a jeep or on camelback. The service is operated by the original Bedouin inhabitants of this area, the legendary, warlike Howeitat tribe, who made a decisive contribution to the victories of Lawrence of Arabia 80 years ago. The tribe has formed a cooperative and offers an excellent fixed-price service.*

38-39 *The Arabs call them* mehari, *while because of their legendary stamina, Europeans have nicknamed them the "ships of the desert". The dromedary, which can be either ridden or used as a pack animal, is inevitably associated with the Bedouins. This animal, capable of travelling up to 31 miles a day and going without water for 10 days, has accompanied and assisted the destiny of man, in the Middle East and in the Sahara, for at least 27 centuries (from perhaps 700 B.C. until a few decades ago). Two events in its history are associated with Jordan. The camel-driver's saddle was invented here by Tamud nomads around 500 B.C., and Salih, the pre-Islamic prophet mentioned in the Koran who forbade his disciples to kill dromedaries, lived here at an unknown period. Now, however, these once invaluable animals are being pensioned off and replaced by jeeps; only 18,000 dromedaries remain in the whole of Jordan. As a result, what was once the "ship of the desert" is now only the third most popular type of transport after motor vehicles (251,000) and donkeys (20,000). The herd of wild dromedaries seen grazing at Wadi Rum in this photo will soon be a thing of the past.*

39 *The rocks of Wadi Rum, especially near springs, are covered with carvings made by inhabitants of the valley in almost 6,000 years of history. The oldest carvings date from the 4th millennium B.C., while the most recent were evidently made only a few decades ago, as cars are portrayed. This photo shows rock paintings of the Tamud period (6th-3rd centuries B.C.), which are some of the oldest in the world portraying caravans of dromedaries. Among the most important carvings in the Wadi Rum area are those of Ayn Ash-Shallalah (known as "Lawrence's spring"), Siq Al-Khazali (the canyon in the mountain of the same name) and Disah (a village where a rock "map" dating from the Copper Age has been found).*

40 *All the Bedouins of the Howeitat tribe, who have always been the "masters" of Wadi Rum, are now sedentary; villages of houses (the largest ones being Rum and Disah) have replaced the traditional black tents.*

41 top *Paradoxes of the desert: 25 miles from Wadi Rum as the crow flies is the Red Sea, and 90 miles away is the Dead Sea (shown in this photo) where holidaymakers swim. There is a big difference in height too: Jebel Rum is the highest point in the country, while the Dead Sea is the lowest.*

41 bottom *Another paradox: thanks to a network of irrigation ditches, green fields of vegetables stand out against the desert. This is Ar-Rashidiyya, the "gateway" to Wadi Rum.*

The River Jordan, the sacred source of green fields

42 top and centre *Bare, arid and mountainous – the area in which Petra is situated at first sight looks impossible to cultivate, yet the Nabataeans, who lived in the city from the 6th century B.C. to the 1st century A.D., were excellent farmers. The Edomites, their predecessors in the region, also possessed famous vineyards.*

42 bottom *The Bedouins of the Liyatneh and Bdul tribes, who still live in the Petra area, consider themselves to be the descendants of the Nabataeans; the guards who protect the archaeological zone of the ancient capital (shown in the photo) are recruited from among them.*

43 *Visitors travel in horse-drawn carriages along the Siq, the spectacular canyon leading to the hollow in which Petra stands, which was once the bed of Wadi Musa, a periodic stream. The Nabataeans diverted the stream by building a dam which, after suitable alterations, is still in operation. The dam, built just before the entrance to the canyon, served two purposes: the former bed of the stream became a paved road, and the water was conveyed to a basin that acted as a storage tank for water used both for drinking and for irrigating the surrounding fields. The Siq dam, believed to have been built in the 1st century A.D., is one of the oldest hydraulic works in Jordan – a courageous experiment designed to make a land in which nature has never been very generous easier to live in and cultivate.*

44 top *This is an area typical of the fertile part of Jordan. The photo was taken near Wadi As-Sir, just outside Amman, looking towards the River Jordan. This is one of the few parts of the country in which water is naturally plentiful. The valley is inhabited by a non-Arab minority, the Circassians, originally from the Caucasus, who emigrated here 150 years ago.*

44 bottom *By far the most fertile part of the country is the Jordan Valley, as demonstrated by these watermelon plantations near Tabaqat Al-Fahl, along the border with Israeli Galilee. Thanks to farms of this kind, Jordan is able to export fruit and vegetables. Among the most economically important items are tomatoes, lentils and potatoes. Tomatoes in particular are grown far in excess of the country's requirements, and the surplus is sold abroad, bringing in precious revenue.*

45 *In an arid country, the presence of water always has a sacred significance. This is particularly true of the River Jordan, whose name evokes numerous Biblical episodes, and also applies to some minor watercourses; Arab tradition has it that Wadi Musa, the Petra river, derives from the spring which, according to the Bible and the Koran, issued forth when Moses struck a rock with his staff. The small Wadi Zarqa (in the photo), which forms some attractive waterfalls before joining the Dead Sea, was once surrounded by an aura of sanctity; the town of Baal-Melon, dedicated to the Canaanite god Baal, stood on its banks, and in Moses' time there was a famous oracle by its waters, which partly issue from hot springs (and are therefore even more "miraculous").*

46-47 *The water of the River Jordan is a source of life, but it has to be used sparingly, as the flow of the river has declined in recent years, causing some areas to dry up.*

46 top *Orchards and fields of vegetables are the characteristic features of the Jordan Valley. The most common type of fruit is mandarin oranges, followed by lemons, apples and bananas.*

46 bottom *Olives, grassy meadows and cereal fields are the characteristic features of the landscape in the north of the country. Fodder production is essential, because rearing livestock (cattle, and above all sheep and goats) is the country's main economic activity in terms of the numbers employed. As a result, the export of dairy products makes a vital contribution to Jordan's economy.*

Aqaba, where sand meets sea

48 *When the summer sun is at its hottest, Aqaba is a dazzling sight, because all the buildings are painted white to repel the heat. In the middle of the picture you can see the ruins of the* qasr *(castle), once the headquarters of the Turkish garrison defeated in 1917 by Lawrence of Arabia and the Howeitat Bedouins.*

49 A harbour (in the background) and tourist beaches (foreground) coexist along the 25 miles coastline on which Aqaba, the only Jordanian town by the sea, is situated.
The resort area, where the most famous hotels are situated, is close to the Israeli border. The last building before the frontier is King Hussein's palace.

Crystal-clear waters

50 top *Huge colonies of gorgonians rise majestically from the parts of the reef most subject to the action of the currents. Their shape is unmistakeable, even from a distance, and although they are a common sight, they always attract divers' attention.*

50 top centre *Turtles are not unusual in these waters, where food is plentiful. Their slow progress attracts the attention of divers, but if they feel threatened, these reptiles can swim off quickly towards the open sea or deeper waters.*

50 bottom centre Chaetodon semilarvatus, *called the masked butterflyfish because of the dark patches around its eyes, is found only in the Red Sea. During the day large numbers of this fish can often be glimpsed in the darker parts of the reef.*

50 bottom *An emperor angelfish (*Pomacanthus imperator*) swims near the sea bed, keeping close to cavities and crevices in the reef where it can hide if threatened.*

50-51 *The wreck of the Cedar Pride, which sank in the spring of 1986 and has now been colonised by underwater flora and fauna, has become a favourite destination for divers swimming in the waters off Aqaba.*

52-53 *The name of the batfish* (Platax orbicularis) *derives from the long fins and dark colour of the juvenile fish. As they grow, they acquire a more rounded shape and a silvery colour with wide stripes of darker or paler shades, according to the fish's condition.*

53 top *Magnificent sea fans decorate the bed of the Red Sea.*

53 top centre *Shoals of jacks are quite frequently found in the column of water in front of the outer wall of the reef. These predators find plenty to eat in this area, on the borderline between the reef and the open sea.*

53 bottom centre *A coral grouper* (Cephalopholis miniata) *stands out on the reef because of its bright red colour with dark flecks. Unlike other groupers, which tend to be shy, this species is often seen out in the open.*

53 bottom *Soft corals are always fascinating, as their translucent colours reveal the delicate inner structure of the colony's branches. The size of these organisms often varies during the day because of their ability to contract and expand when they absorb water.*

53

In the shadow
of temples and minarets

54 top *Present-day Jerash is the ancient Gerasa, once a stronghold of the Roman Decapolis. The large Imperial ruins are separated from the modern town by a river (Wadi Jerash) crossed by a pair of bridges.*

54 bottom *As-Salt (or Salt) has only 40,000 inhabitants, but an impressive history; founded in the Iron Age, it was the capital of Petraea in Biblical times, and became a stronghold of resistance against the Crusaders in the 13th century.*

55 *Amman once stood on seven hills (Jebel), which have now become 19, because the present-day capital has nearly 2 million inhabitants. In the heart of the city stands the Mosque of Hussein (shown in the photo), rebuilt in 1924. This monument is dedicated to the Hashemite Emir Hussein I, hero of the Arab rebellion, who formed an alliance with the British during the First World War, armed the Bedouins and contributed to the defeat of the Ottoman Empire. After the war Hussein kept the present Saudi Arabia for himself, and gave Transjordan to his son Abdullah, grandfather of the present King Hussein II.*

56-57 *Amman, like Jerash, has a Roman past; during that period it was called Philadelphia, and was also part of Decapolis. Imperial ruins still stand among the houses of the modern town, and the Roman theatre, with a capacity of 6,000 spectators, is still used today. This impressive building was erected in the 2nd century A.D., probably during the reign of the Emperor Antoninus Pius. However, the origins of the city are not Roman. Amman already existed in Biblical times; it was the capital of the Ammonites, with the name of Rabbath Ammon. It then became Israelite, then Ammonite again, and was subsequently conquered in turn by the Assyrians, the Babylonians, the Ptolemies of Egypt, the Seleucids of Syria and finally, the Nabataeans. It was not until 30 B.C., when it already had at least 2,000 years of history, that the present capital of Jordan joined the Roman Empire; it was conquered for Rome by Herod the Great, the King of the Jews referred to in the Gospels. The Ammonites, after whom the city was named, were a Canaanite people, mentioned in the Bible. They had a love-hate relationship with the Jews; they were enemies of the Jewish King Saul, but allies of Solomon (970-931 B.C.). Defeated and scattered by the Babylonian King Nebuchadnezzar, they disappeared from history in the 6th century B.C.*

57 top *In Roman times Amman developed considerably as a result of its position on the road leading from Bosra (in Syria) down to Petra (the present King's Highway). Little now remains of the Forum, which was so large that it became legendary; the most evident trace is this row of columns which was part of a portico surrounding the square on three sides, while the fourth was bounded by a small river (now underground), the Seil Amman.*

57 centre *The oldest part of Amman stood on the hillside now called Jebel Al-Qalah or Citadel. On the summit there was a site consecrated to the local deities, which the Roman conquerors replaced with a temple dedicated to Hercules (shown in this photo). It was built by Emperor Marcus Aurelius (A.D. 161-180), who decorated it with impressive statues and a majestic staircase.*

57 bottom *The Odeon, another place of entertainment dating from the Imperial age, is much smaller than the Roman theatre; it held only 500 spectators. It was also used for open-air concerts.*

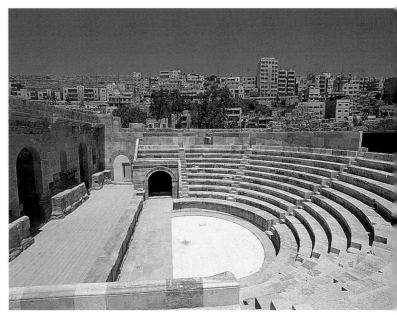

58-59 *The capital of Jordan is now an orderly modern metropolis, despite the population explosion which has multiplied its size. The headquarters of King, government and parliament, it recently became a major business centre, and a meeting point for Western and Arab society. Although it is overcrowded (at least a third of the entire Jordanian population lives here), the traffic flows more smoothly in Amman than in many European cities thanks to the wide boulevards at the foot of the hills; the most central is Shari Al-Amanah (shown in the photo), which runs right in front of the Mosque of Hussein.*

59 top *One of the symbols of modern Amman is the Al-Malik Abdullah Mosque, unmistakable with its two minarets and blue majolica-clad dome. The building, which dominates the skyline to the north-west of the city centre, was completed in 1990. The contrast between ancient monuments and ultra-modern buildings, with no trace of intermediate stages, is one of the most characteristic features of Jordan's capital. After the splendours of the past, Amman fell into decline, and was totally abandoned from the 13th century until 1920, when it was "refounded" as a result of a decision taken round the conference table.*

59 bottom *At a panoramic point on the top of Jebel Ashrafiyah, to the south of the city centre, stands another characteristic modern monument, the Mosque of Abu Dervish. The large number of mosques reflects the importance of the majority religion, Sunnite Islam. There are also some Christian minorities in Jordan, especially Melkite, Greek Orthodox and Armenian groups, mainly in Amman.*

60-61 *In accordance with the Arab custom of not reproducing the human figure (which is not laid down in the Koran, as is commonly believed), Jordanian Islamic monuments have no statues or frescoes, and Amman is no exception to the rule. As a result the architects' imagination has run riot in the use of arabesques, colour combinations and plays of light and shade. A typical example of this trend is the Mosque of Abu Dervish, the decoration of which is based on two-tone effects.*

61 top right *The National Archaeological Museum contains finds from all over the country, including the Balua Stone, the Citadel Heads and the Dead Sea*

61 left *Numerous statues of different periods, from the Neolithic to the Roman period, are housed in the National Archaeological Museum in Amman. An excellent example is this head of a woman which dates from around the 2nd century A.D., when ancient Philadelphia reached the height of its development. The head was found by chance during excavations in the museum's own garden.*

61 bottom right *Although the Mosque of Hussein was founded in the 7th century by Caliph Omar Ibn al Khattab and rebuilt in the Twenties, it owes its present appearance to the renovation work completed by King Hussein II in 1987.*

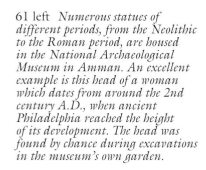

Scrolls. The Balua Stone, which dates from the 13th century B.C., depicts Moabite deities, while the Citadel Heads are two-headed columns dating from the 7th century B.C., which were found in the oldest part of Amman. The Dead Sea Scrolls are part of the huge "library" left by the Jewish sect of the Essenes in the caves of Khirbat Qumran (West Bank). Many of the scrolls are now in Jerusalem, however.

62 top *Aqaba, like Amman, has a long and glorious history, though few traces of it now remain. The city, which may be the Biblical Ezion-Gever, the port of King Solomon, prospered in the early centuries of Islam under the name of Ayla – "a Palestinian port on a branch of the China Sea" as it was described by Arab geographer Shams Ad-Din Muqaddasi (10th century). The heart of the old town is the* qasr *(fort), with the coat of arms of the Hashemite royal family over the entrance.*

62 centre *Numerous wall inscriptions commemorate the history of the fort of Aqaba. The most prominent states that it was built by Emir Khayir Bey al-Ala'i during the reign of Sultan Qansaw al-Ghawri (1501-1516), "scourge of unbelievers and polytheists". However, there is no*

doubt that a Crusader castle already existed on the same site.

62 bottom *The entrance to Aqaba castle arouses inexpressible emotions in Jordan citizens; this is where the rebel Howeitat Bedouins entered in August 1917, when they conquered the stronghold of the Turkish occupiers. The storming of Aqaba castle was the sign that the revolt of the Arabs against the Ottoman Empire was destined to succeed, and that independence was within their grasp.*

62-63 *Historically important, a symbol of power and once considered impregnable, the fort of Aqaba is actually little more than a redoubt (measuring barely 538 feet square). In the past, the building was used as a shelter by pilgrims on their way to Mecca.*

64-65 *Modern Aqaba is something of a paradox. For half a century it lived "at war" with neighbouring Eilat (shown in the background of this photo), the Israeli outpost on the Red Sea, yet the two towns, which are only a couple of miles apart, have almost always observed an unspoken pact of non-belligerence – in fact, not a shot was fired here in the 1973 war. This is even more surprising in view of the fact that the majority of the inhabitants of Aqaba are Palestinian. A double boundary fence runs between the two cities; until 1994 the border could not be crossed, but there is now a frontier post (called Arabah by the Jordanians and Arabà by the Israelis).*

65 top *Even during the period of hostilities with Israel, Aqaba has always been a holiday resort. There is a long row of luxury hotels along the sea front, like the Coral Beach (shown in the photo).*

65 bottom *Aqaba earns even more revenue from its harbour (the only one in Jordan and one of the most important on the Red Sea) than from tourism. This is the terminus of the Hejaz railway, which brings tons of phosphate from the mines of the interior to the docks. Aqaba is now preparing for the post-oil era; not far from the harbour are the headquarters of the Royal Scientific Society, which is experimenting with the use of solar energy to desalinate sea water.*

66-67 *Tourism has begun to develop in Aqaba since the recent peace with Israel, as a result of investments by large international hotel chains. The Holiday Inn International can be seen in this photo.*

68-69 *Numerous hotels have also been built by the Dead Sea, to exploit the curative properties of the region's mud.*

People of fields and camels

70 top *Bedouins resting in the desert, not far from Petra. The red-and-white* keffiyeh *is the usual headgear of the indigenous population, the white one may be worn during a festival or as a mark of social distinction, while the black-and-white* keffiyeh *is generally worn by Jordanians of Palestinian descent.*

70 bottom *The donkey is still a very common means of transport, at least for short journeys. There are 20,000 donkeys in Jordan; more than the number of camels.*

71 *This tea vendor in Irbid is wearing a* fez *instead of a* keffiyeh. *The* fez *is a hat of Turkish origin, which is now seldom worn. The method of making coffee inherited from the Ottoman empire is still very common, however: the coffee beans are ground very finely, boiled in water together with sugar, and often flavoured with cardamom.*

72 top *"Give the right measure and be not fraudulent: let your scales always be correct"*, recites the Koran in sura (chapter) XXVI, called the *"Chapter of the Poets"*. It is no accident that the sacred book of Islam devotes some specific precepts to trade; accustomed for centuries to living on trade between distant countries, all Arabs have business in their blood. You can't say you really know an Arab town until you've been to the suk, the local market, and Amman is no exception; its suk, a riot of colours, perfumes and voices, is situated around the Mosque of Hussein.

72 bottom *Another place where negotiations are typically conducted is the coffee house, where people usually don't drink coffee at all, but* chai *(aromatic tea, nearly always mint-flavoured); there's plenty of time to talk about business between cups of* chai.

73 top *Peasants often come in from the countryside to sell their produce in the* suk.

73 bottom *The silhouettes of high-rise blocks built in the last 30 years can be glimpsed behind the stalls of the* suk; *the capital of Jordan is like that, a portrait of ancient rituals in a modern frame.*

74-75 *Of the five* arkan *(the duties of every good Muslim), the most important is faith, followed by prayer – preferably in the mosque, and better still, collective. So at midday every Friday, the Islamic day of rest, the Mosque of Hussein in Amman fills with worshippers; there's such a crowd that even the square in front of the mosque is packed. The vast majority of Jordanians (96%) are Sunnite Muslims; they are usually very devout, but also extremely tolerant of non-Muslims.*

76 top *A chat in the open air is a pleasure, an opportunity for socialising that Jordanians rarely miss. The favourite meeting time is the evening, when the temperature is at its most pleasant. The rule is that groups consist of all men or all women. Anywhere will do as a meeting place; the one chosen by this group of women, the beach at Aqaba, is rather unusual, as Jordan has few beaches, but the climate on the coast (mild in winter and very pleasant in spring and autumn) is very tempting. The mean temperature in Aqaba is 15.6°C in January (the coldest month), 24.3° in April, 27.1° in October and 22.1° in November. In midsummer it's warm, though not as hot as might be expected; only the month of August is really sweltering, with an average of 33°C.*

76 bottom *When the high season is over and the tourists have left Aqaba, you're likely to see more people wearing* keffiyehs *than swimsuits on the Red Sea beach. This isn't surprising in view of the fact that the desert begins less than 3 miles away, behind the first mountain chain, and you never undress in the desert. The Jordanians are not seafaring people; only 24 tons of fish a year are caught, which puts Jordan last of all the countries bordering on the Red Sea. To get an idea of what this figure means, Egypt and Yemen respectively earn 12,000 and 45,000 times more from fishing than the Jordanian landlubbers, great-grandchildren of the Nabataeans.*

77 *This beach terminates in another country – Israel. That's just one of the paradoxes of the Western districts of Aqaba, the most popular with bathers. Until 1994 launches flying opposing flags cruised off this shore, eyeing each other warily from a close distance, and swimmers risked colliding with the row of buoys marking the border between the territorial waters of the two countries, officially enemies. Nowadays the* atmosphere *is much more relaxed; military launches are more unusual, the beaches are more crowded, and the only national flags are flown by tourists' yachts, shaded by frivolous sun blinds. The "Peace Games", a kind of local mini-Olympics, where Jordanians and Israelis challenge each other to swimming, windsurfing and rowing races, are held in these waters in November to celebrate King Hussein's birthday.*

78 top *Some of the most popular souvenirs in Jordan are bottles full of coloured sand.*

78 bottom *The art of making bottles of sand reaches levels of rare perfection, giving work mainly to younger people.*

79 *As Arab culture considers it improper to reproduce the human figure, the artistic skills of the Jordanians run riot in costume jewellery, carpet weaving, glass making and pottery. Here again, their distant but deep-rooted Nabataean heritage emerges. The inhabitants of Petra were considered some of the best potters in the known world, so it comes as no surprise to find that the decorations of modern ceramics, the patterns woven into carpets often reproduce ancient ornamental motifs.*

80 *Mosaic art is another very ancient tradition, which still survives in Madaba, a town world-famous for its mosaic decorations from the Byzantine period. So that this tradition can be handed down to future generations, a mosaic school (shown in the photo) has been opened at the local Church of the Virgin, and will soon be moving to a period building. This mosaic art, which not only reproduces arabesques but also portrays people and animals, is perhaps enhanced by the fact that a Christian community lives in Madaba; the town has four more churches apart from the Church of the Virgin.*

81 In Jordan, even glassware has distant origins. This craftsman, who lives on the slopes of Mount Nebo (Jebel Nuba) probably does not know it, but his working methods are not very different from those of the master glassmakers whose exquisite products were used from Syria to the Red Sea in the Abbasid and Fatimid period (A.D. 750-1071). Some pieces dating from that period, which were found among the ruins of mediaeval Ayla, are now on display in the Aqaba Archaeological Museum. The products made by the craftsman from Mount Nebo will end up on the stall of a suk, at least until the passing of time turns them into antiques.

82 *"And out of the ground made the Lord God to grow every tree that is pleasant to the sight, and good for food; the tree of life also in the midst of the garden, and the tree of knowledge of good and evil. And a river went out of Eden to water the garden...."* That is how the Book of Genesis describes Eden, the garden of delights, which had everything that the Semitic people, used to the aridity of the desert, could wish for. Perhaps the writer of Genesis had the Jordan Valley in mind; it has a river that waters the fields, and the tree of good and evil, which an ancient tradition identifies with the apple tree. However, the Jordanian orchards (shown in this photo) are not those of the Garden of Eden, which grew spontaneously; man has had to work hard to obtain trees like these. And more still remains to be done, because fruit picking and maintenance is nearly all performed by hand even now.

83 top left *Although Koranic law prohibits Muslims from drinking alcohol, not all Jordanians are Muslims, and the Koran does not prohibit the production of wine for sale to "infidel" populations. As a result, 5,000 hectares of the Jordan Valley are given over to vineyards, mainly growing white grapes. Thanks to these vines, which are of excellent quality (the best being situated near Salt), Jordan produces 50,000 tons of grapes a year; some are eaten fresh, and some are used by the wine-making industry, which produces very good quality wines. Vine-growing, like the crafts already mentioned, is an ancient tradition in Jordan; the Edomites, who lived in the Petra area between the first and second millennium B.C., were skilled vine-dressers.*

83 top right *The main agriculture produce is tomatoes, and the tomato harvest gives work to a large number of seasonal pickers, as in the rest of Europe. Nearly all tomato growing is concentrated in the Jordan Valley (shown in the photo), where tomato plantations cover a quarter of the fertile land (10,000 hectares out of 40,000), and give several harvests a year. Tomatoes are the staple ingredient of several dishes typical of Jordanian cuisine, such as* daud pasha *(meatballs made of lamb with onion, pine nuts, rice and tomatoes). Much of the country's produce, which is of excellent quality, is exported, mainly to other Arab countries. Trade with Europe is on a smaller scale because Italy tends to overproduce, so that tomatoes are a glut on the market.*

83 bottom left *Although it has had to tackle all sorts of problems in the course of its short existence, Jordan has not neglected environmental protection. A government agency (the Royal Jordanian Society for the Conservation of Nature) currently operates three nature reserves: two (Azraq and Shawmari) in the eastern desert and one (Dana) to the west, between Petra and Al-Karak. As it is situated on the migration route between Turkey and the Nile Valley, Jordan is particularly important for birds (300 species have been recorded). Mammals which still live wild in the country include the wolf (*Canis lupus*), the fox (*Vulpes arabica*), the caracal (*Felis caracal*), the Nubian ibex (*Capra ibex nubiana*) and the reintroduced Arabian oryx (*Oryx leucoryx*), whose offspring are tagged one by one (see photo) and monitored by the park rangers.*

83 bottom right *The Arabian oryx (*Oryx leucoryx*), called* maha *by the Arabs, is a magnificent antelope once common throughout the Middle East, which the Bedouins regard as a symbol of independence. With its long straight horns, white coat and black face, the* maha *is a desert specialist; it can go without water for 11 months, and cover 90 miles a day in search of food. It died out in Jordan in the Twenties, and is seriously endangered in the rest of the world, but a recent repopulation plan for the species seems to have encountered a degree of success; the Shawmari Wildlife Reserve in the eastern desert is now home to several dozen oryx. Apart from Shawmari, herds of oryx live wild in the desert of Jiddat Al-Harasis (Oman), and Israel also has a few dozen specimens in the enclosed Hai-Bar Yotvata reserve (Negev).*

84 *A train of dromedaries driven by Bedouins files past the impressive ramparts of Wadi Rum. But this is not a caravan heading for distant countries, only an excursion for tourists, with Bedouins acting as guides. In a country where everything is still linked to tradition, the greatest changes of lifestyle in the last few decades have been those of the Bedouins, although they are the most jealous custodians of the ancient traditions. Nomadism, which was the normal way of life for the majority of the population at the turn of the century, has declined rapidly; although over 50% of the population are of Bedouin descent, there are now no more than 50,000 true nomads. It is not unusual nowadays for former camel drivers to work in another field that involves moving around – they are employed as guides, truck drivers and soldiers, and even as taxi drivers.*

85 *Bedouins rarely ride their camels; the camel-driver usually walks in front of the animals, which are laden with goods and baggage. Pictures like this one, which were common a few decades ago, are now becoming increasingly unusual; dromedaries are now only used for transport in the most uneven terrain, where not even a modern 4WD vehicle can venture. However, dromedaries are still a source of wealth for the desert tribes, who obtain milk and wool from them; a herd of dromedaries is still a valuable asset.*

86-87 *A Bedouin on his camel is an image that fires the imagination, evoking romantic dreams and suggesting pride, freedom and dignified self-sufficiency, even if the Bedouin, like this one, is wearing the olive-green uniform of the Desert Police Patrol. The Hashemite monarchy recruits soldiers for the élite corps from among the former desert nomads, especially the Howeitat tribe, which has been loyal to the Royal family since the days of Hussein I, when they rebelled against the Turks on the Emir's orders. The bodyguards of the present King, Hussein II, are also Howeitat Bedouins. The Jordanian Bedouins, close "cousins" of the Bedouins of the Sinai and Saudi Arabia, believe that they are descended from a single common ancestor called Miriam. However, her descendants are divided into various tribes; other tribes present in Jordan, apart from the Howeitat, are the Beni Attiya (in the Al-Karak area), Beni Khalid (to the west), Lyatneh (around Petra) and Al-Sirhan (in the north). Oddly enough, one tribe is called Al-Issa, which literally means "of Jesus".*

A legend called history

88 top *Jerash is the Pompeii of Jordan – an ancient Roman city which can still be discerned almost in its entirety. Unlike the real Pompeii, however, the houses no longer exist, because there was no eruption to "freeze" them for centuries. The ancient Gerasa went into a slow decline, like many cities in the world, and the people used its blocks of stone for new buildings erected elsewhere. However, the plan of the ancient city has now clearly emerged from the land; colonnades and temples are still in place, and the theatres are still used.*

88 bottom *Qalat Ar-Rabad is a mediaeval Arab castle that towers over the city of Ajlun, in the north. Stout and well equipped, it symbolises Muslim resistance against attacks by the Crusaders. It was built in the 12th century by Emir Izz Ad-Dim Usama, who paid tribute to the legendary Sultan Saladin.*

89 *Of all the archaeological sites in Jordan, none is as famous as Petra, and Al-Khaznah (shown in this photo) is perhaps its best-loved symbol. Here, more than anywhere else, Jordanian history began. In pre-Roman times Petra was the capital of the Nabataeans, who founded a highly original civilisation in the desert; although it was based on nomadism, they created a great capital, consisting of monuments excavated in the rock.*

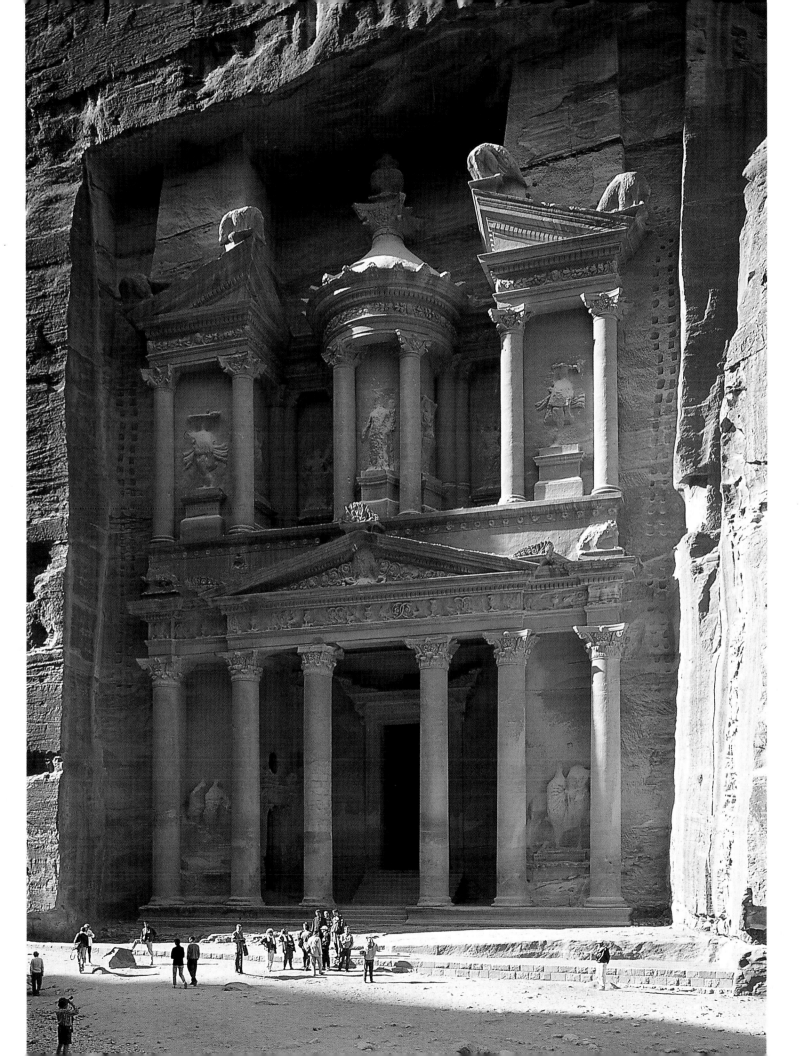

Petra, the ancient heart of the Arabs

90-91 Disquieting, impressive, in perfectly harmony with the rock face that frames it: ad-Deir, the most famous monument of Petra, stands apart from the rest of the city on a hill, solitary as only a king can and must be. In fact, ad-Deir was to have been dedicated to a king; Rabel II, Nabataean King of Petra from A.D. 71, intended to be buried there. Amid the silence of the Mounts of Edom, where no-one but the god Dushara was allowed to speak, his people would venerate him forever.

91 top right Petra did not only consist of tombs; the "outer Siq" is overlooked by the remains of a theatre incorrectly called the "Roman Theatre", which was actually built by King Aretas IV (A.D. 9-40).

91 bottom right On a hill called Madhbah, once used for sacrifices, two 20-feet-tall obelisks still stand; they may have been dedicated to Dushara, god of the mountains and sun, and his wife Allat, goddess of the morning star (Venus).

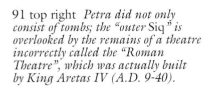

So he had this unparalleled 150-feet tall monument excavated; the tholos alone (the round sanctuary on the façade) was 30 feet tall. However, his dream of peace and grandeur was destined never to come true. Before Dushara called him to eternal rest, Rabel II, King of the desert, was defeated by the Roman invaders, and his kingdom became a foreign province. That was in A.D. 106; all that now remains of the last Nabataean King is an empty temple, watching over the desert.

91 left It takes nearly an hour to walk from Petra up to the Mausoleum of ad-Deir, following a mountain trail into which steps have been cut in places. Various Nabataean tombs excavated in the rock face can be seen on the way; the most attractive is the "Lion Triclinium", so called because two stone lions stand guard over the entrance.

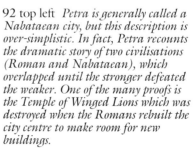

92 top left *Petra is generally called a Nabataean city, but this description is over-simplistic. In fact, Petra recounts the dramatic story of two civilisations (Roman and Nabataean), which overlapped until the stronger defeated the weaker. One of the many proofs is the Temple of Winged Lions which was destroyed when the Romans rebuilt the city centre to make room for new buildings.*

92 centre left *The Tomb of the Roman Soldier (2nd century A.D.) is post-Nabataean, although it was adapted to suit Roman taste.*

92 bottom left *The Tomb of the Obelisks (A.D. 40-71) is important because it demonstrates the level of Petra's international relations; the external architecture betrays Egyptian influences, while the interior contains an bilingual inscription in Greek and Nabataean.*

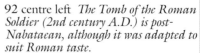

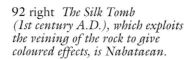

92 right *The Silk Tomb (1st century A.D.), which exploits the veining of the rock to give coloured effects, is Nabataean.*

92-93 *The Cardo Maximus, one of the main roads of Roman towns, was built during the reign of the Emperor Trajan (A.D. 98-117), and redesigned the centre of Petra with porticoes and colonnades.*

94-95 *In this aerial view of the centre of Petra, the Monumental Gate built by the Romans in the 2nd century A.D. can clearly be seen in the foreground; this is the starting point of the Wadi Musa valley. The mountain in the background (Jebel Al-Khubthah) is riddled with Nabataean royal tombs.*

96 top *The triple Urn Tomb, with an impressive façade supported by a double row of arches, stands out on the face of Jebel Al-Khubthah. This tomb, which dates from the reign of Malichos II (A.D. 40-71), was destined for an important person, perhaps the King himself. After the fall of the Nabataeans the tomb was converted to other uses; in the Byzantine period it was a Christian church.*

96 top centre *If you look at Petra from above, you will see something odd; many of the monuments are built high up, around the edge of the town, while the central valleys are emptier. There's a good reason for this. The stone monuments are nearly all mausoleums and temples, hence their elevated position; however, little remains of the "city of the living", which was situated further down, because it consisted largely of tents, as might be expected for the capital of a people of nomadic merchants.*

96 bottom centre *Qasr Al-Bint is one of the very few monuments built of stone, as opposed to being excavated in rock. It seems certain that it dates from the reign of Aretas IV (A.D. 9-40), but its function is unclear; the current theory is that it was a temple of Dushara.*

96 bottom *Apart from royal tombs, there are numerous "minor" burial places in Petra, excavated in the rock like those of the kings. The largest necropolises include the one around the Theatre and the one at the entrance to the Siq.*

96-97 *This may not be the most attractive, but is certainly one of the most impressive of the mausoleums bordering the rock faces of Jebel Al-Khubthah. It is built on three superimposed levels, and is therefore called the Palace Tomb. It may have been built in the early years A.D., but the exact date is uncertain.*

98-99 *Ad-Deir, which stands alone outside the town, is the loveliest of the 800 monuments of Petra, which is why it was chosen a few years ago, together with Al-Khaznah, as the location for a film in the "Indiana Jones" series. Seen from the top of Jebel Harun, the highest mountain in the region, the mausoleum of Rabel II looks less impressive, just a tiny dot amid deserted mountains against the background of the Arabah Valley, which is why it is called ad-Deir (the Hermitage).*

100-101 *Legend has it that Al-Khaznah (the Treasure) contains the treasure of an Egyptian Pharaoh. The story obviously isn't true, but everything about Al-Khaznah is mysterious: its function (temple or mausoleum?), its builder and its date. Some experts attribute it to King Aretas III (84-56 B.C.), others to Aretas IV (A.D. 9-40), while others date it from the reign of Roman Emperor Hadrian (A.D. 117-138).*

101 left *The fortunes of Al-Khaznah are partly due to its position; the monument stands at the end of the Siq, producing an unrivalled surprise effect. However, the "Treasure" is also justly famous for its sophisticated architecture. The monument is reached by crossing a vestibule and climbing a short staircase.*

101 top right *Al-Khaznah is richly decorated, at least on the outside. The façade has 12 columns with Corinthian capitals.*

101 bottom right *On the façade of Al-Khaznah, there are three doors beyond the vestibule which lead to two hypogea and a central chamber. The latter, as severe and bare as the façade is rich in decoration, has a number of niches in the walls; at first sight they appear to be burial places, but this theory has never been proved.*

102 *The technical skill of the unknown architects of Petra's tombs often reached outstanding heights; they even exploited the natural veining in the rock faces to obtain colour effects of rare beauty. The interior of this tomb is one example, but the masterpiece of this kind is the Silk Tomb, which has coloured streaks on the façade ranging from pink to turquoise.*

103 top left *Another example of natural colour decoration in a tomb; the composition of the rock, a friable sandstone with warm, soft shades, made the architects' task easier.*

103 bottom left *The interior of the tombs of Petra generally consisted of huge empty chambers with large niches in the walls, where the bodies were placed.*

103 top right *The most important of the non-royal mausoleums is the Tomb of Aneishu, which evokes the last years of the Nabataean kingdom. Aneishu was a minister who managed to keep Petra independent at a very delicate time. The story begins in A.D. 70 , when the expanding Roman Empire decided to punish the rebellious Jews on the opposite side of the Ghor, and Jerusalem was destroyed. Nabataean King Malkus III helped the Romans, but shortly afterwards he died, leaving the city to an heir who was not old enough to rule. Aneishu took power together with the King's mother Shuqailat, and the two regents held the fort, managing to keep the Romans at bay until the King came of age. However the young King Rabel II proved not to be as skilful as Aneishu, and years later, an exile in the desert, he left Petra to the legions of Rome.*

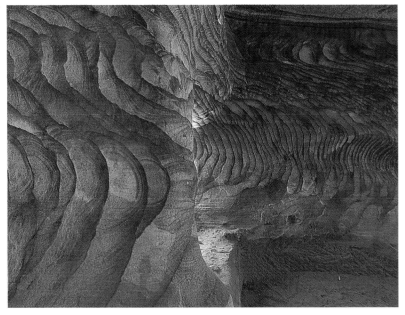

103 bottom right *The interior of some of the tombs at Petra is so spacious and tidy that the local Bedouins used them as semi-permanent residences for centuries, until very recently. In 1812, when Swiss traveller Johann Ludwig Burckhardt rediscovered the "rose-red city", the cavities of the Outer Siq were still inhabited by shepherds from the Lyatneh tribe, and some tombs had even been converted to stables. Most of this "occupation" lasted until the 1960s and 1970s, when King Hussein had a modern rural village built to the north of the archaeological area, ordered all the "homeless" to move to the new settlement, and began restoration work on the monuments. Now, only a few tombs on the slopes of Jebel Ras Suleyman, outside the perimeter of the town and off the normal tourist routes, are still used as sheep folds.*

104-105 *"Aaron shall be gathered unto his people: for he shall not enter into the land which I have given unto the children of Israel, because ye rebelled against my word at the water of Meribah. Take Aaron and Eleazar his son, and bring them up unto mount Hor: and strip Aaron of his garments, and put them upon Eleazar his son: and Aaron shall be gathered unto his people, and shall die there." According to the Bible, this is how God announced the last day of Aaron, brother of Moses and high priest of the Jewish exodus. According to the Biblical account, Mount Hor stood on the border of the country of Edom, ie. in the Petra region, and Arab tradition identifies it with Jebel Harun, the highest peak in the vicinity. On the top stands a small white mausoleum where Muslims, oddly enough, venerate the Jewish priest, considered to be the forerunner of Mohammed because he was the prophet of monotheism.*

105 top *Jebel Harun is reached in a five-hour walk from the centre of Petra. It is not known when the mausoleum on the summit was built; the building resembles numerous other sanctuaries in the Islamic world dedicated to prophets and saints.*

105 centre *According to the Bible story, when Aaron died, the Israelites had already reached the border of Canaan. In fact, Jebel Harun overlooks the Arabah Valley, the depression below sea level beyond which lies present-day Israel.*

105 bottom *Sunset on the heights of ad-Deir is one of the loveliest sights that Petra has to offer, because of the peaceful situation, the view, and the symbolic significance of the whole picture; ad-Deir was the last monument of Nabataean Petra, and marked the decline of this extraordinary civilisation of kings in the desert.*

Jerash, where the empire prevailed

106 top *The city now called Jerash was once known as Gerasa, pearl of Decapolis, the complex of 10 cities that constituted the outpost of the Roman Empire in the Middle East. Impressive, vast and well kept, the ruins of Jerash are to Roman Jordan as Petra is to Nabataean Jordan. The Temple of Zeus (shown in this photo), high above the Forum, is the equivalent of ad-Deir in the "rose-red city" of the desert – a symbolic monument that combines the maximum architectural skill of a civilisation with the authority that only the supreme divinity can inspire. Founded by the soldiers of Alexander the Great, perhaps in 332 B.C., Gerasa became Roman in A.D. 90, and reached the height of its glory in the 3rd century. A Temple of Zeus already existed in the 1st century, but the present building is later, perhaps dating from 163.*

106 bottom *From the top of the Temple of Zeus you don't look out over the desert, as at ad-Deir, but onto an elliptical Forum from which the Cardo Maximus, the main road of the city, begins. The views of Petra are light years away; there, the city was adapted to the mountain, imaginatively exploiting its rock faces, valleys and even its colours, whereas here, a hyper-rational geometrical design was imposed on the land, even modifying its colours to the standard pinkish-grey of the blocks of stone. A comparison of Petra and Jerash clearly shows the revolution that took place in Jordan after the Roman conquest; the heart of the country moved from the caravan routes to the cities, from south to north, from the silence of the caravanserai to the busy social life of the Forum and the Basilica.*

107 *On the slopes of the hill sacred to Zeus, on the opposite side of the Forum, stands the South Theatre, built in the reign of Domitian (A.D. 81-96). The building, which once seated 5,000 (now only 3,000), has perfect acoustics and is still used for open-air performances, especially during the Jerash Festival, held every July. The South Theatre was the largest, but not the only one in ancient Gerasa; the remains of the North Theatre, built in the 2nd century in a less central position, which had a capacity of 1,600, can still be seen. The presence of two buildings of this kind demonstrates the level of cultural and social sophistication reached by the city, which is no doubt why the Emperor Hadrian, who loved the East, chose Gerasa as his favourite residence in 130.*

108 left *The patron goddess of Gerasa was Artemis (Diana), and a large temple, built in the 2nd century on an open space right in the middle of the city, was dedicated to the huntress of the Greek/Roman Olympus. The building must have been magnificent, but its remains are mutilated, because it was often renovated and used for other purposes over the centuries; for example, it became a kind of market specialising in ceramic ware in Byzantine times.*

108 right *Gerasa entered a decline in the 3rd century, but city life still continued in later times, as demonstrated by the numerous early Christian and Byzantine churches scattered among the pagan temples. The oldest is the Cathedral, built in the second half of the 4th century on the site of an earlier temple dedicated to Dionysus.*

108-109 *The Temple of Artemis was surrounded by a Corinthian colonnade; the remains of its columns demonstrate that its perimeter measured 525 x 394 feet.*

110-111 *The impressive Cardo Maximus crossed the whole city, from the Forum to the North Gate, following a straight route less than a mile long. This main road of ancient Gerasa was lined with 260 columns on either side, which once supported majestic porticoes.*

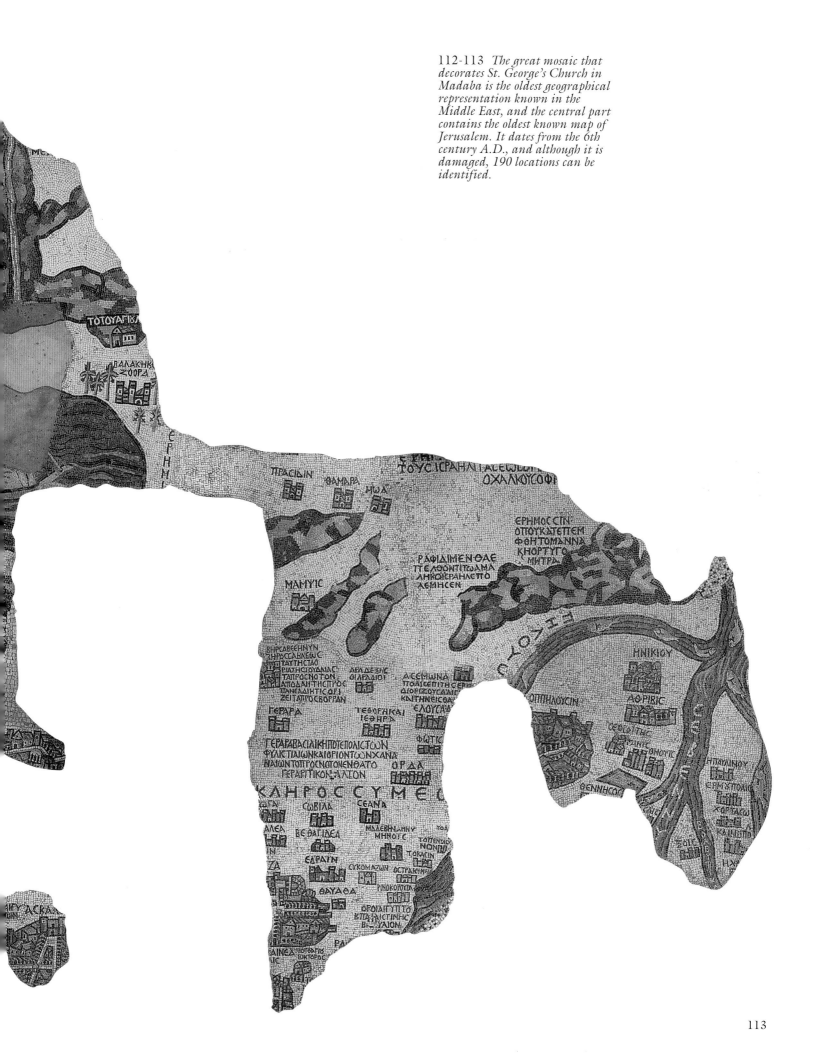

Madaba, the royal art of mosaic

114 *The "Map of Palestine" is not an isolated curiosity. Madaba, a city with a large Christian Arab population, is world-famous, like Istanbul and Ravenna, for its mosaics, which decorate four different churches. The head of Christ shown in this photo is in the Church of the Virgin.*

115 top left *A school of mosaic art is still based in the Church of the Virgin.*

115 bottom left *The mosaics in the Church of the Virgin at Madaba are generally well preserved, apart from the "historical" damage caused by the iconoclasts. The main subjects are saints and martyrs.*

115 top right *Decorations inspired by plants, like those with vine and acanthus leaves, frequently appear in the mosaics at the Church of the Virgin.*

115 bottom right *This mosaic in the Church of the Virgin portrays a 6th-century house.*

116 top *Mosaics, the greatest expression of Byzantine art in Jordan, are found not only in Madaba, but all over the surrounding area. The village of Khirbet Mukayyet, not far from the capital, is particularly interesting, because the 6th-century Byzantine church, destroyed and abandoned for centuries but excavated in the Thirties, has some exquisite mosaic floors (shown in the photo). Oddly enough, this church is dedicated to "Saints Lot and Procopius". Lot is actually a Biblical character who, according to Jewish tradition, was far from saintly; according to the account in the Book of Genesis, he committed incest with his daughters. These unorthodox relationships led to the birth of the Moabites, a race considered to be sinners and idolaters. The Moabites are known to have lived in the region where Madaba is situated today, and it is strange that a church in this area should be dedicated to Lot, their legendary ancestor.*

116 centre *This overall view of the interior of the church of SS. Lot and Procopius at Khirbet Mukayyet shows the wealth of mosaic decoration with plant motifs. Note that the pattern closely resembles that of certain traditional Arab carpets.*

116 bottom *Visitors who continue beyond Mukayyet can climb to the top of Mount Nebo (Jebel Nuba), where the Diaconicon (a vestry reserved for deacons in ancient times) has a surprise in store: a 6th-century carpet with hunting scenes, whose style recalls the mosaic of Khirbet Mukayyet. Unusually, the carpet bears the date of manufacture (531), and the names of the makers, Elia and Soclo Kaiomo. The carpet provides some interesting information about the way various populations dressed at the time.*

117 top *Mount Nebo is a very popular destination, but those who climb to the top are not only interested in the famous carpet. Tradition has it that Moses was buried on the summit at the end of the Jewish exodus. Oddly enough, however, Mount Nebo is only venerated by Muslims and Christians, while Jews have always been indifferent to it. There is a Christian monastery on the summit (the first nucleus of which dates back at least as far as the 4th century). In the past the monastery was run by Egyptian monks, but it is now in the care of by the Franciscan Order. So how did the tradition originate? There is obviously no proof that Moses is really buried here, but there are some remarkable coincidences with the Biblical account. According to Deuteronomy, "... Moses went up from the plains of Moab unto the mountain of Nebo, to the top of Pisgah, that is over against Jericho. And the Lord shewed him all the land ... So Moses the servant of the Lord died there ...he buried him in a valley in the land of Moab, over against Beth-Peor: but no man knoweth of his sepulchre unto this day." The name of the mountain tallies, and so do the geographical references; Jericho is about 20 miles away, and the plain of Moab is even closer. However, the Biblical version says that Moses' tomb was "in a valley", not on the mountain.*

117 centre *There are some exquisite Byzantine mosaics on Mount Nebo too, like this elegant peacock surrounded by vine shoots.*

117 bottom *The interior of the Mount Nebo monastery as it is today, after renovation work carried out in the Thirties; the foundations and shafts of the columns of the older church, which was destroyed, have been covered by a modern canopy. The location of the alleged tomb of Moses is marked by a cross.*

Castles
of war
and faith

118-119 *Those who travel south along the King's Highway will encounter a stout fortress, about halfway along the route between Amman and Petra, which commands the plateau from its strategic position at a height of just over 3,000 feet. This is the castle of Al-Karak, built by the Crusaders in 1132 on the orders of Baldwin I, King of Jerusalem, but occupied in 1189 by Saladin's Muslims. Jordan was torn apart by religious wars for centuries, first between Muslims and Byzantines, then between Crusaders and Muslims. Islam arrived here a few years after Mohammed's death, and the Byzantines were defeated in 636. When the first Crusaders arrived in 1096, total war broke out, until Saladin conquered the whole of what is now Jordan for Islam in 1187. The fortress of Al-Karak, used alternately by armies of opposing faiths, is not the only relic of those times; the whole of the centre-north is studded with castles (qasr). However, not all of them were built during the period of the Crusades; some date from long before Islam, and even from pre-Christian times.*

119 top *The walls of Al-Karak tell tales of deeds both chivalrous and murderous. The lords of the castle included not only Baldwin IV, who signed a treaty with the Muslims to guarantee the safety of pilgrims of both religions, but also Reginald of Châtillon, who used to throw prisoners over the precipice.*

119 centre *North-east of Amman, on the Syrian border, stand the ruins of Umm Al-Jimal, a city which flourished during the first two centuries of Islam under the Omayyad caliphs. It was destroyed not by the Crusaders, but by an earthquake.*

119 bottom *As demonstrated by the ruins of a water tank, the Omayyads went to a great deal of trouble to convey drinking water through pipes to Umm Al-Jimal, which had no springs.*

120-121 *Four towers and walls built with 20-ton stones; Qasr Al-Abd must have been practically impregnable before the invention of artillery. However this castle, situated at Araq Al-Amir near Amman, has nothing to do with the Crusades, and was probably never used for war at all. This is the only Jordanian qasr to date from pre-Christian times; it was built in the 2nd century B.C., during the Hellenistic period. But who could have had any interest in building a castle of this kind at the time? The builder of Qasr Al-Abd was Hyrcanus, a member of the noble Tobiad family from the Amman region, which managed to benefit from the partition of Alexander the Great's conquests. In fact, while the two great Hellenistic kingdoms (the Ptolemies of Egypt and the Seleucids of Syria) fought to gain the upper hand in the Middle East, the provincial lords of the Tobiad family created a fiefdom in North Jordan, and struck an alliance with the Ptolemies. This small kingdom on the borders of Syria had great strategic importance for Egypt, so the Tobiads became untouchable. Qasr Al-Abd was built more to impress their powerful neighbours to the north than to be used in war, but it was a pointless task, and in fact the building was never finished.*

121 top *The interior of Qasr Al-Abd, which was never completed and partly destroyed by an earthquake, is not easy to interpret. The buildings enclosed within the walls were erected on two floors and equipped with a water tank. Some interesting reliefs decorating the walls depict animals (especially felines).*

121 bottom *This view of Qasr Al-Abd shows the very unwarlike appearance of the castle, which was not built on a hill as usual, but in a depression. The building originally seems to have been surrounded by a small lake, of which no trace remains. In place of the lake there is a boundary wall, which was added to the original castle in the Byzantine period.*

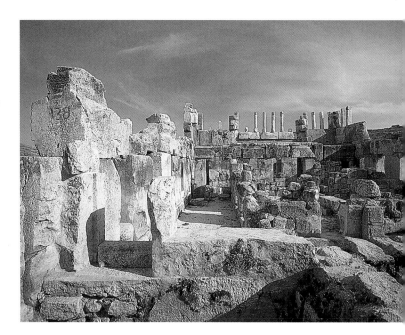

122 top *The ruins of the Church of Ash-Shawbak (or Shobak), on the King's Highway not far north of Petra, date back to the period of the Crusades, which was far more warlike than the time of Hyrcanus. These crumbling walls stand at the entrance to a mighty castle built in 1119, like that of Al-Karak, by the Christian King of Jerusalem Baldwin I.*

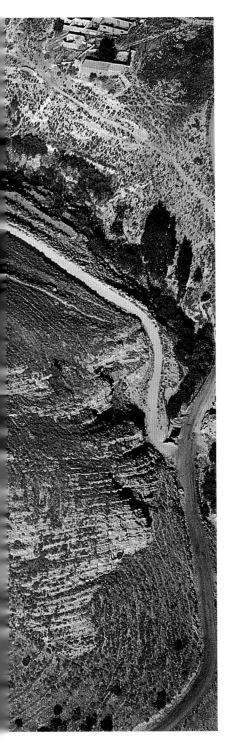

122-123 *The castle of Ash-Shawbak stands on a hill overlooking the Arabah Valley, in such a dominant position that the Crusaders called it* Mons Regalis, *and the name has survived to the present day. The fortress formed a single defensive unit with Al-Karak, with which it communicated by a beacon system. Like Al-Karak, it was besieged and taken by Sultan Saladin in 1189. After falling into Muslim hands, the castle was renovated by the Mamelukes (13th-14th centuries). One of its most unusual features is a well excavated in the rock with 375 steps, leading to the tank that supplied water to the garrison.*

123 top *The small museum in the castle of Ash-Shawbak contains various mediaeval objects found in the area.*

123 centre *Unlike the previous castle, Qasr Al-Kharanah is of Muslim origin. It was almost certainly built by the Omayyads, caliphs in the early decades of Islam. According to a wall inscription (whose authenticity is doubted by some experts) it dates from the year 711. Qasr Al-Kharanah, which stands guard over a place to the east of Amman where desert trails cross, was certainly used as a caravanserai as well as serving as a garrison.*

123 bottom *Inside, Qasr Al-Kharanah can clearly be seen to have served as a caravanserai (a stopover for caravans); apart from accommodation for people, it also had stables for animals.*

124 top *Most of what remains of Qasr Amrah is occupied by the throne room, where the Caliph received guests who visited him when he was there on holiday. Large, elegant archways support the vaulted ceiling, dividing it into naves.*

124 centre top *The interior of Qasr Amrah holds a surprise: the walls and vaults are all frescoed, and not with arabesques. Scenes of hunting, work and private life are painted on the walls. This is very unusual in the Islamic Arab world, which has always considered it improper to reproduce the human figure. Some of the frescoes at Qasr Amrah even show naked women bathing. In fact, this is not a wholly isolated case; frescoes showing human figures are also found in the Arab palaces of Granada (Spain), for example. In both cases, they are a sign of a progressive, liberal court that appreciated the pleasures of life, art and culture, as the Arabs of Spain and the Omayyads certainly did.*

124 centre bottom *The fortress of Machaerus on the hill of Al-Mishhaqah dates from the time of Herod the Great (37-4 B.C.) and Herod Antipas (4 B.C. to A.D. 39), and is associated with a famous episode from the Gospels; it was here that the second Herod imprisoned and then killed John the Baptist.*

124 bottom *Qasr Al-Mushatta, near Amman, is another elegant Omayyad castle; once richly decorated, it has been stripped to fill German museums.*

124-125 *Lost in the deserts of the east, towards Azraq, is one of the most fascinating "castles" of the Omayyad period. It is called Qasr Amrah, but it looks nothing like a fortress; it has no towers or boundary wall. However, what we see was part of a larger complex that also included a fort, now destroyed. In fact, Qasr Amrah was not built for military purposes, but as a hunting lodge for Caliph Walid I (705-715).*

Umm Qays and Pella, archaeology in progress

126-127 There is still much to be discovered in Jordan, a country which already has a rich archaeological heritage, and many of the treasures excavated in the past 20 years still remain to be studied in detail. The country invests a large amount of resources in excavation, but a major contribution is also made by specialist foreign institutes, which collaborate with the Department of Antiquities in Amman. A joint venture with Sydney University led to the discovery, starting in 1979, of the ruins of ancient Pella, founded by Alexander the Great and later incorporated into the Roman Decapolis. So far the remains of a Roman theatre and a basilica (shown in this photo) have been uncovered, and excavations are continuing.

127 top The small village of Tabaqat al-Fahl, scarcely marked on the maps, was unaware until 20 years ago that it was the ancient Pella, and had capitals like this one buried in the subsoil.

127 centre The history of Gadara, another city of the Decapolis, resembles that of Pella. After disappearing from history and the maps for centuries, Gadara is now re-emerging near the village of Umm Qays, in the far north of Jordan; excavations which began in 1973 in collaboration with the German Evangelical School in Jerusalem are still continuing. The monuments uncovered include the colonnade of a basilica.

127 bottom At Umm Qays, the ancient Gadara, urgent restoration work needs to be carried out on the theatre, which could be used today, like the one in Jerash.

128 Qasr Al-Abd, the "folly" built by the Tobiad Hyrcanus near Amman, was not uncovered by excavations; its unfinished bulk and the reliefs portraying various felines (shown in this photo) have always been known to the inhabitants of Araq Al-Amir, a suburb of the capital. However, studies are also in progress here, this time with French collaboration, and will perhaps find an explanation for what appears to be a folly, built by the Lord of Amman.

All the pictures are of Massimo Borchi / White Star except for the following:

Antonio Attini / Archivio White Star: pages 42 top and centre, 70, 89.

Marcello Bertinetti / Archivio White Star: pages 50, 52, 53.

Angelo Tondini / Focus Team: pages 22-23

Vincenzo Paolillo: pages 50-51.

Padre Piccirillo: pages 112-113.